HOW TO HAVE AN *Awesome* ADVENTURE

This edition published in 2019
By SJG Publishing, HP22 6NF, UK

Author: Helen Redding
Illustrator: Josy Bloggs
Cover design: Milestone Creative

ISBN: 978-1-911517-79-5

Printed in China

10 9 8 7 6 5 4 3 2 1

CONTENTS

"Ships are safest when they are in port.
But that's not what the ships were built for."
Anon

INTRODUCTION

It's very easy to get stuck in a rut. We work hard day in day out, the same routine – there's a danger that every day starts to feel identical. If boredom sets in, what can you do? Have an adventure! It's these adventures that this book explores; the many ways in which you can shake up your life a little (or a lot) and inject it with a dose of excitement.

Some of the ideas might seem a bit too far out of your comfort zone. But remember that everyone's idea of 'adventure' is different – start small and shift your boundaries inch by inch if that's what you're more comfortable with. If you are ready to bungee off a bridge attached to a piece of elastic, then go for it. Choose an adventure that is right for you, and you'll be rewarded with an enormous sense of achievement.

So use the ideas and advice in this book to cultivate your spirit of adventure – who knows where it will take you?

WHAT'S *your adventure?*

We can all get an itch that makes us want to break out of the routine of our everyday lives. An urge to try something completely different, to do something wild or to overcome a long-held fear. You need an awesome adventure to scratch that itch! Adventure means different things to different people, so here are some ideas to help you pinpoint what makes you buzz …

MAKE A BUCKET LIST

Not sure what adventure you have in mind? Make a bucket list. Don't be limited by the unrealistic or the mundane! Get all of your ideas down on paper and you'll find new ideas emerge that you have never considered before. Let your imagination be sparked and your sense of adventure will be truly set alight.

DREAM (QUITE!) BIG

Dream big, but be realistic. If you are paying off debts, then handing in your notice and heading off around the world might not be a good idea. Adventures don't have to be grand, so think about what would give you a buzz but that can be done within your current restraints. Boring – that's life! – but it doesn't mean you have to miss out.

WHAT DO YOU ENJOY?

What adventures have you enjoyed in the past? What did you vow that you'd never do again? You don't have to go outside your comfort zone to get a sense of achievement. Perhaps you love hiking and love France but have never combined the two – make an adventure of a hobby by doing it somewhere new. If you hate camping, don't plan anything that involves a tent. It's about pleasure, not pain!

BRAIN OR BRAWN?

Would you like your adventure to be physical, cultural or maybe spiritual? If you're looking to challenge your body, white water rafting or climbing could be for you. A cultural adventure could take you off the beaten track in a country you've long dreamed of visiting. To explore your spiritual side, a retreat off the grid might be your ideal unplugged adventure. Or combine physical and spiritual, and scale a mountain and meditate at the peak!

WHAT MAKES YOUR HEART PUMP?

It is not all about adrenaline and thrill-seeking. Your pulse
might soar when you taste your favorite wine in the region
where it was grown. Literature loves might swoon walking in
the footsteps of a beloved author. The thrill of the new could
determine your adventure; or perhaps revisiting people
and experiences could rekindle the fun you had on a past
adventure.

FIND INSPIRATION

So, you've tried making a bucket list, but you're still stuck for an idea for an adventure, and that itch needs scratching! It's a nice but frustrating problem to have. Try some of these ideas for finding inspiration …

FIVE GREAT SOURCES OF INSPIRATION

1. Get down to your local library and browse the travel section for other people's adventure stories.

2. Read blogs. There are blogs galore on the internet about personal journeys and experiences. Get busy with your trusty search engine to investigate.

3. Read the news. Newspapers and websites love stories of people taking on challenges big and small. Browse the news to see what other people have done – something could spark your own ideas.

4. Read some classic adventure stories. It could be fiction: Around the World in 80 Days, The Beach or The Swiss Family Robinson. It might be non-fiction, such as Elizabeth Gilbert's journey of personal discovery in Eat Pray Love.

5. Research rainforest explorers, ocean swimmers, polar adventurers and circumnavigators of the globe. Seek out amazing achievements to fill you with energy even if you're not aiming so big! People overcome all kinds of obstacles to follow a dream, and there's no reason why you can't.

HELP! I'M STILL STUCK!

Don't despair! Just because you can't come up with an idea, it doesn't mean you're not cut out for adventure. Ask your friends and family for their ideas – what would they do if they had the chance? Plus, ask them what they think you should do. Other people can have a very different perspective of you than you do of yourself, and they may have some genius ideas that you hadn't even considered.

INSPIRATIONAL MODERN-DAY ADVENTURERS

Emily Chappell
extreme adventure cyclist

Benoit Lecomte
swam the Atlantic Ocean

Martin Strel
swam the entire length of the Amazon River

Mirna Valerio
ultramarathon runner

Sarah Marquis
solo traveler

Beverly Joubert
conservation filmmaker and photographer

Alastair Humphreys
micro-adventurer finding adventures in everyday life

Emily Woodhouse
extreme adventure knitter

Lee Humphries
aiming to stand on the highest point of 100 countries around the world

ARE YOU AN
awesome adventurer?

Everyone's definition of adventure is different – because everyone is different! You might not have the adrenaline-seeking genes that make you want to base jump off a skyscraper. Equally, the thought of an adventure on your doorstep might send you straight to sleep. What qualities do you need to enjoy your awesome adventure?

Adventurous /əd'vɛntʃ(ə)rəs/ (adj.) ~
willing to take risks or to try out new methods, ideas or experiences.

THE ADVENTUROUS PERSONALITY TYPE

Does this sound like you?

- throws caution to the wind
- challenges their boundaries and restrictions
- non-conformist – has their own code of values
- independent
- good at influencing and persuading others
- loves to keep moving and exploring
- courageous, bold and tough
- lives in the present
- ventures where others fear to tread.

Doesn't sound anything like you? Don't panic! Everyone is cut out for some kind of adventure. Putting aside the action and derring-do, do you:

- ✓ like learning new things
- ✓ know when you're bored
- ✓ enjoy dreaming
- ✓ learn quickly
- ✓ tackle new experiences, even if you're scared?

How to Have an Awesome Adventure

Answer 'yes' to any of these, and you're just as ready for adventure as the crazy kid with the backpack heading for the remotest place on Earth. Choose your adventure to suit your personality. If you've never traveled abroad and an adventure for you means going to the next town on the bus – so be it! – go to that next town.

Don't let the fact that you're not James Bond or Bear Grylls stop you from creating your own awesome adventure. Work within your own boundaries and sense of comfort, but remember that if you push those boundaries – even a little – you'll build the confidence to make your next adventure slightly bigger and slightly scarier. And you'll grab it by the horns and enjoy it!

OVERCOME YOUR FEARS /
What's stopping you?

Whatever the size of your adventure, if you're feeling a little daunted you may find excuses to put it off or not do it at all. Overcoming those obstacles and excuses is all part of the journey. After all, we'd never have got to the Moon if we'd dismissed it as being a bit too tricky.

MONEY, MONEY, MONEY

Unless you're lucky enough to have won the lottery, money and financial commitments are bound to be a consideration when planning an awesome adventure. Even the smallest of adventures may require money you don't have at hand. But while you need to be realistic and not build up debts, money shouldn't stop you from following your dreams:

- Save, save, save. There's no need to rush your adventure. Planning (and saving) is all part of the fun.
- Could you earn money from your adventure? (See page 79.)
- Could you take a sabbatical from your job, giving you the security of a salary to return to?

FRIENDS AND FAMILY

Even the most independent and self-sufficient of adventurers miss their friends and family. If you're going away, it's important to have the support of your loved ones and to plan in advance how to keep in touch (see 'Keeping a record of your adventure', page 82). That way, everyone will feel part of your adventure and know you're safe. Likewise, you'll be reassured that everyone at home is okay. If your adventure is small but you feel like you're achieving big, then tell people! You'll be surprised at how much support you'll get. Just knowing that people are rooting for you can provide an enormous confidence boost. Be proud of your awesome adventure.

THE FEAR FACTOR

"What if I fall?" Oh but my darling, what if you fly? – Erin Hanson

Are you scared of the experiences and feelings your adventure might bring? Don't worry – that's entirely normal. Even the hardiest of adventurers worry – if they didn't, then they wouldn't be able to plan against the risks. Successful adventures aren't about recklessness! If you're overly risk-assessing and this is stopping you from even getting started, then make a list of what could go wrong and try these steps:

- On a scale of 1–10, how real are those risks? Are you imagining obstacles that aren't there?
- If the risks are real, what can you do to limit them? (E.g. enlist a friend for support, have a back-up plan, etc.)
- Think about how you'd feel if those obstacles weren't an issue. Excited? Confident? Powerful?

PLAN, PLAN, PLAN

Throwing caution to the wind might seem the spirit of the true adventurer, but in reality, planning is key to making your adventure as awesome as possible. If you're not comfortable just winging it, then you need to get organized, get focused and get planning.

"A goal without a plan is just a wish."
Antoine de Saint-Exupéry

THE FIVE BIG Qs

Where? What? When? How much?
And make sure you can answer 'Why?'!
If you can't, then perhaps it's time to go back to the drawing board. What makes your adventure awesome is what the experience means to you. Don't jump out of a plane just because Johnny next door has done it and you're jealous of the attention he got.

PLANNER
Things to Do
Get Travel Jabs
Sort Mobile Phone Network
Check Exchange rate
Currency
Emergency cash

CHECKLIST
☐ Passport
☐ Visa
☐ Tickets
☐ Travel
☐ Insurance
☐ Money
☐ Health Ins

TOP FIVE PLANNING TIPS

1 Research – with the internet at your fingertips, there's no excuse for not getting the lowdown on what to expect.

2 Know your limitations, and plan for and around them. (See 'What's stopping you?' page 14.)

3 Write it down! You might think you can keep it all in your head, but you need to clear space in that brain of yours, so get key information down on paper or in a spreadsheet.

4 Don't leave planning until the last minute. No matter how big or small your adventure, get thinking about it well in advance, put your plan in place and then sit back and enjoy the anticipation.

5 Planning an adventure should be positive and fun, so if you feel yourself getting overwhelmed, take a step back and have a break.

THE BORING
PRACTICAL CHECKLIST

✓ Can you afford it? Do you need to factor in some time to save money?

✓ Do you need vaccinations and visas? Is your passport valid?

✓ Have you got travel insurance?

✓ What equipment and clothing do you need?

✓ What help do you need from other people? E.g. catching a lift somewhere, borrowing equipment, introductions to contacts.

Remember – even the best-laid plans are not 100% fool proof. Accept that you can't plan for every eventuality, and give yourself permission to make mistakes. Be prepared for things to change, and just think of the attributes you'll then be able to add to your resumé: flexible, adaptable, able to work well under pressure …!

GOING *solo*

Going on an awesome adventure requires bravery. Doing it alone requires bravery and a dash of courage on top! While the idea of embarking on an awesome adventure alone can be scary, conquering that fear could be the beginning of the ultimate journey.

TOP REASONS TO GO IT ALONE

1. Your adventure is a very personal journey. Maybe it's to reconnect with a lost loved one. Perhaps you have a phobia to conquer. It's you versus the world, and you feel more comfortable doing it by yourself.

2. Too many cooks spoil the broth. You have very specific ideas about your adventure and, quite frankly, anyone else tagging along inserting their own ideas would just ruin it.

3. Logistically, if there's just one person to look after, things get a whole lot easier!

19

How to Have an Awesome Adventure

4 No one wants to do it with you. So, do it on your own and show everyone what they've missed! Plus, you're more likely to meet new people if you are by yourself.

5 You need to get away from it all, disconnect from routine, devices and other people. This isn't selfish – it can sometimes be very necessary.

6 Going solo and achieving a dream is incredibly empowering.

SELF-INDULGE

There is something deliciously self-indulgent about doing things on your own. Even if it's just whiling away time in a coffee shop, the pleasure is in the fact that you're in control and making the decisions. No one is telling you to hurry up and drink your coffee because they want to do something else. A solo adventure is no different. It's a chance for you to focus solely on yourself and really get a sense of what you're capable of. This applies whether it's a personal challenge like learning a new language or a big backpacking adventure around the world.

BEST COUNTRIES FOR SOLO TRAVEL

According to Travelandleisure.com, the top 10 safest (and happiest) countries to travel alone in are:

1 New Zealand
2 Norway
3 Switzerland
4 Costa Rica
5 Austria

6 Vietnam
7 Chile
8 Japan
9 Sweden
10 Indonesia

21

How to Have an Awesome Adventure

SOLO BUT NOT ALONE

If you want to be a solo adventurer but are anxious about traveling alone, joining a group trip is an ideal solution.
It is a great way of wading into the world of traveling, and can be a stepping stone towards going out on your own. You will get all the perks of being by yourself (single accommodation, spending downtime alone if you want to) but with added benefits – a ready-made group of like-minded people to support you and give you a cheer when you achieve something awesome.

INCREDIBLE SOLO ADVENTURERS

These amazing people dreamt big (you don't have to go this big!) and achieved their dreams solo:

Jean Batten (b.1909):
first person to fly between England and New Zealand solo.

Erden Eruç (b.1961):
completed the longest solo ocean row of 312 days, rowing the Pacific from east to west.

Felicity Aston (b.1977):
first woman to cross the Antarctic solo.

Krystyna Chojnowska-Liskiewicz (b.1936):
first woman to sail solo around the world.

Hannah Engelkamp:
spent six months walking 1,000 miles around Wales with a donkey called Chico.

SAFETY TIPS

Keeping your wits about you, your guard up and using your common sense will stand you in good stead for awesome solo adventuring. Here are a few useful additional tips:

- Stay connected. Keep your cell phone charged so that you have a lifeline.

- Let people know where you're going regularly and when you expect to return – including friends and family back home and your hotel/host.

- Keep your money, credit cards and passport in separate places.

- Research your destination. Be aware of local customs and etiquette. Find out which areas to avoid after dark.

- Ensure your accommodation is safe. Keep your door locked, ideally stay off the ground floor and get a room close to busier areas.

- Stay healthy and seek help quickly if you think you're unwell.

KEEP IT IN THE FAMILY

Who said the adventures stop when you have kids? Family adventures are a great way to enjoy experiences together, create lasting memories and bond. Sure, there are extra factors to consider to ensure it works for the whole family, but don't let that stop you seeking out an awesome adventure!

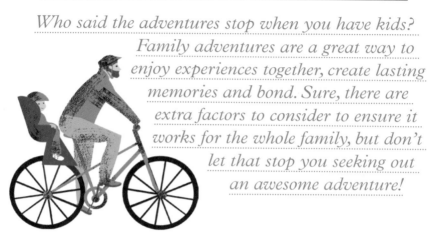

GO FOR IT!

Your children are never too young. A newborn is very easy to take on an adventure – they're not bothered where they are, as long as you meet their need for food and sleep. Toddlers are a bit trickier, but give them the outdoors and they discover a great big playground. Tweens and teens? They'll be difficult anywhere, so you might as well give in to them Instagramming their adventure and keep them happy.

Shhh, don't tell the children, but an adventure is educational. The world is a brilliant teacher. Learning about history, geography, science and the arts becomes so much more interesting when you're learning firsthand rather than from books.

How to Have an Awesome Adventure

A family adventure is a brilliant way to share things – that includes the ups and the downs. We spend so much of our time in different places, that coming together every so often lets you reconnect and build strong bonds. Children crave adventure, and parents need to roll their sleeves up and show them how it's done!

An adventure boosts everyone's confidence. It is a great way to introduce your children to new things and learn new skills. Dealing with the challenges of an adventure is perfect for developing your children's character and resilience.

SMALL BUT GREAT ADVENTURES

A family adventure can start close to home (and they don't all cost money). Try these:

- Clean a beach (or organize a litter pick with your neighbors).
- Enter a race or challenge together.
- Go geocaching.
- Go on an outdoor scavenger hunt.
- Stargaze away from the bright lights.
- Camp in the backyard.
- Be everyday explorers – turn down a path you've never walked along and see where it leads you.
- Go to theme parks.

VERY BIG ADVENTURES

If you want to go further afield, make sure you know what will suit your family (before you spend big bucks):

Multi activity:
Kayaking, canoeing, cycling, walking, rafting, surfing … the list goes on, but they all keep everyone active.
DO: If you can't sit still.
DON'T: If you're all couch potatoes.

Wildlife:
Go on safari in Botswana, snorkel with sea turtles in Costa Rica, spot wild elephants in Sri Lanka.
DO: If your kids love animals (and they're patient!).
DON'T: If you don't do creepy crawlies or early starts.

Walking:
If you're adventuring by foot, plan for all the legs in the family.
Energetic teenagers might be happy walking all day, but if you want to avoid lots of whining, littler legs will need shorter trots and more interesting stops.
DO: If you love the great outdoors.
DON'T: If the closest you own to walking boots is a pair of Converse.

Road trips (see page 53):

An amazing way to see more and do it under your own steam. Tailor the adventure to your family's interests and keep everyone (more or less) happy. DO: If you love the call of the open road.

DON'T: If your children get horrendously car sick.

Single-base trips:

If you can't bear the thought of continually packing and unpacking bags, then base your family in one spot with plenty of adventures within easy reach.

DO: If you love coming back after a busy day to a cool beer at your favorite table.

DON'T: If the same families and their same squawking children at breakfast every morning fills you with dread.

Big adventures

Great – you're lucky enough to be thinking BIG! If it's a dream of a lifetime you're planning, it's going to be enormous fun to plan and to, well … DO.

Think Indiana Jones throwing his satchel and whip in the back of a rusty plane; think selling all of your belongings and living in a remote yurt on the Mongolian steppe. These might sound unrealistic – maybe they'll need tweaking a bit to come within your budget and skillset – but if you want a really big adventure, then you've got to dream a little to make it happen. Here are some jaw dropping ideas to get you started …

"Dr Livingstone I presume." It's over 160 years since the explorer David Livingstone set off down the Zambezi river in search of what the locals called 'the smoke that thunders'. To this day, Victoria Falls remains one of the must-visit sights in the world – in fact, it's one of the Seven Natural Wonders. The Falls are around 5,577 feet wide and up to a height of 304 feet. You may not be venturing into the unknown as Livingstone was, but if you want something spectacular that will leave you speechless then this could be the adventure for you.

Climb Kilimanjaro – all 19,340 feet of it. Head to the roof of Africa and look down in awe across Kenya. A fantastic challenge if you're wanting to push your physical limits, but also ideal if you've not got technical climbing experience. Let's face it, anyone will be impressed by this accomplishment (they don't need to know it's 10,000 feet shorter than Everest …).

Bored of running 5 km, 10 km, half marathons and full marathons? Need a really challenging adventure to test your running prowess? How about entering the Marathon des Sables? Described as the toughest footrace on Earth, this ultramarathon (yes, six times the distance of a regular marathon) will take you across the Sahara Desert for 6 days, covering 251km. This is not for the faint hearted, but we are talking about BIG adventures here. And it's not just one for the youngsters – British adventurer Sir Ranulph Fiennes completed the race in 2015 at the age of 71!

How to Have an Awesome Adventure

Campervans give you the ultimate freedom to travel at your own leisure. The world is your oyster, so where could a campervan take you? New Zealand is a firm favorite for adventurers by road, providing amazing volcanic landscapes, mountains, beaches and rugged coastlines, wildlife and fantastic cultural experiences. Alternatively, stay closer to home and explore your own country – maybe trace its coastline or tick off all of its national parks. Stop, see, enjoy and then hit the road again.

If two wheels are more your style, then pack a puncture kit and head off on a cycling adventure. Whether it's a physical challenge you are after or you would prefer just to pootle along with a bunch of flowers in your basket, there's a bike trip out there for you. How about the North American Great Divide mountain bike route? This off-road route takes you all the way from Alberta in Canada to New Mexico – a mere 2,700 miles! If you're a Sunday afternoon cyclist, then this might not be the adventure for you – even if you do get to see mountains, forests and the Colorado Rockies. Try something a bit more leisurely like the 500 miles 'Road of the Great Wines' in Burgundy, France, where your biggest challenge will be which wine to pair with your cheese.

Is yoga your passion? Why not make a pilgrimage to the birthplace of yoga – India. A great way to combine your sense of adventure with your spiritual quest. There's a list of places to visit as long as your yoga-sculpted arm – try Rishikesh, the 'yoga capital' of North India, full of classes, retreats and new friends for life. If it was good enough for The Beatles in 1968, it's good enough for you! The annual Parmarth **Niketan** International Yoga Festival in Rishikesh brings together swamis and yogis from all over the world to discuss yoga, practice and chant.

A big adventure doesn't need to be physically demanding. If you're a foodie, then plan a trip to exercise your taste buds! There are so many exciting places to visit where you will taste food like you've never tasted before. Where do you want your taste buds to take you? Hunt out the restaurants boasting the top chefs, find out where locals like to eat and book on culinary courses where you can learn to cook like you've lived there all your life. It will truly be an adventure that you can bring home and enjoy over and over again, providing you can find the ingredients!

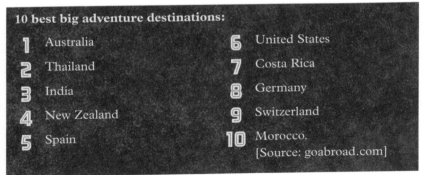

10 best big adventure destinations:

1. Australia
2. Thailand
3. India
4. New Zealand
5. Spain
6. United States
7. Costa Rica
8. Germany
9. Switzerland
10. Morocco.
   [Source: goabroad.com]

EVERYDAY *adventures*

Say 'adventure' and most people tend to imagine traversing continents, or slinging on a backpack and doing Asia on a shoestring. But what about the everyday adventures, like those little things we can do in our lives that make our hearts flutter or our chests swell with pride?

WHAT IS A MICRO-ADVENTURE?

Also known as micro-adventures, everyday adventures are quick, easy and inexpensive to fit into our lives – but just as awesome as big adventures. "Adventure is about enthusiasm, ambition, open-mindedness, and curiosity … adventure is not only crossing deserts and climbing mountains; adventure can be found everywhere, every day, and it is up to us to seek it out … It's for people with real jobs and real lives, with a couple of kids and a cat to feed." – Alastair Humphreys, explorer and author of Micro-adventures

BREAK WITH THE NORM

They say a change is as good as a rest. Doing something different or differently can make you feel more energetic. There's so much in our lives that is safe and predictable – adventure is that feeling you get when you don't know what is going to happen next. Here are some incredibly easy ways to inject some fun and everyday adventure into your life and break out of a rut:

- Try something on that you wouldn't normally wear. Then buy it!
- Visit a friend in another city.
- Enter an obstacle race.
- Put yourself forward for something at work.
- Revisit forgotten skills, for example a musical instrument.
- Make the first move.

- Take a new route to work.
- Camp in your backyard.
- Paint your nails 'this season's color', even if it's beyond bold.
- Say 'yes!' to an invitation that you would usually decline.
- Book yourself on an evening course to learn something you've always been fascinated by.

33

BE GOOD TO YOURSELF

Bored? Restless? Lethargic? Feeling trapped? Everyday and micro-adventures might just be for fun, but they have enormous benefits to your well-being:

- release creativity
- boost your feelgood hormones
- give a fresh perspective
- conquer fears
- beat stress
- distract from everyday hassles.

THE NEXT LEVEL

If you've tried breaking the norm and enjoyed it then, it could be time to take your adventure up a notch. Here are some ideas to shake things up even more, and be invigorated by a dash of spontaneity:

- Be ready for anything! Keep boots in your car, and if you find yourself driving through somewhere beautiful, park up, jump out and go for a walk. You could even keep your swimsuit and a towel in the trunk and indulge in some spontaneous wild swimming.
- End of the week and feeling a bit restless? Grab some friends and a tent and head to a local campsite. Take the bare minimum to get by, and just enjoy the great outdoors with great company.

- Jump in your car or on your bike, and simply roam with no plan. Turn a corner you've not turned before or choose a location you've not been to before, and see what you can discover.
- Book cheap last-minute flights and escape for a weekend. Don't plan where you want to go – just see what's available in your budget and hit the skies.
- Ditch dinnertime at home, pack a picnic from what's in the fridge and find somewhere to watch the sunset. Beautiful.

FIND A SAFE SPACE

The best thing about an everyday adventure is that it can be as tiny as you like. If you don't feel courageous enough to think big, then this adventure gives you permission to start small and still feel awesome. Transatlantic sailors don't jump straight onboard and voyage into the unknown – they learn to sail a boat first! An everyday adventure is your chance to push your boundaries just a smidgeon, to see if next time you could give them a great big shove. Be slightly bold, be a touch brave – but always be awesome.

MAKE A
weekend of it

Big adventures, micro-adventures – but how about something in between? A weekend is a small but perfectly formed way to cram in some fun. It can be near or far, cheap or expensive, deeply daring or surprisingly spontaneous. How would you pack an awesome adventure into two days?

ON YOUR OWN...

- Clear your diary, switch off electronic devices, stock up on food and stay in your PJs. Banish all thoughts of chores and the words "I should ...".
- Binge watch your favorite TV show or movies (or both – you've got the whole weekend!).
- Visit your favorite gallery or museum, and spend time lingering at the exhibits you love.
- Book yourself a weekend course on something you've always wanted to try.
- Pamper yourself – everyone deserves time for self-care!

WITH KIDS...

- Stay in a forest lodge – explore, kick leaves, build dens and spot wildlife.
- Head to a beach for endless ice cream and sandcastles.
- Book a farm stay – fresh air, space to run and animals – the perfect combination for wearing out even the most energetic children.
- Learn a new activity as a family over a weekend. Try paddle boarding, kayaking or keep it dry with a weekend releasing your arty side.
- Spend a weekend on horseback enjoying the slower pace of life on instructor-led hacks.
- Maximize the thrills with an overnight stay at a theme park.

WITH THE LOVE OF YOUR LIFE...

- Take a trip down memory lane to where you first met.
- Recreate your first date.
- Spend a weekend revisiting your favorite restaurants and bars.
- Replay an awesome romantic weekend you've already had, and get the tingles all over again.
- Get married or renew your vows in a wedding chapel in Las Vegas!

WITH NO MONEY...

- Rediscover your local library and spend the weekend under a blanket chilling out with borrowed books, magazines and boxsets.
- Make the most of your neighborhood park and fill your weekend with picnics, community sports and free events.
- Switch off your electronic devices and plan a board games weekend that gets everyone reconnecting and firmly out of the virtual world.
- Take a hike or exercise in the open air, and get your feel-good hormones going.
- Donate your time to a community project and give something back.

WITH YOUR BEST FRIEND...

- Enjoy a relaxing spa weekend – book yourselves in somewhere lush or recreate the experience with DIY treatments at home.
- Go on an epic shopping expedition. Hit the shops early to avoid the crowds, grab some lunch and then head for a night out ... ideally wearing your purchases.
- Stay up all night talking about all the things you're usually too embarrassed or nervous to admit!
- Hit the voucher and discount websites, and book a fancy restaurant that would normally be out of your price range.
- Compile a playlist together, turn up the tunes and take a road trip to somewhere you've never been before.

MAKE THE MOST OF YOUR AWESOME WEEKEND

Plan. Don't try to fill every minute. Allot some downtime. Avoid routine. Get your chores done by Thursday night. Work can wait until Monday – avoid checking work emails. Plan something to banish the Sunday night blues.

ADVENTURES IN YOUR
own backyard

The opportunity for an awesome adventure is often right under our noses, yet we don't even realize it. Take time to stop in your busy life, look around and see what you're missing on your doorstep. You'll be amazed what you've taken for granted all this time.

GET YOUR TOURIST HAT ON ...

With the right mindset and a bit of thought, being a tourist rather than a local is easier than you think:

- Make a list of what tourists do when they visit your town – you may be surprised how much you've never done.
- Check out what discounts on admission fees, tickets, etc. are offered exclusively to residents.
- Ditch the car and take a walk. Look out for places and signs that you don't spot while traveling at speed.
- Stop recycling the leaflets and What's On guides that arrive in your mailbox. Start taking note of the events they're telling you about!

MOUNTAIN
TRAIN TICKET
— $5 —

40

CLASSIC TOURIST TRAIL

Museums and galleries: Most towns have a museum or gallery, no matter how small. Sometimes the most obscure can be the most fascinating, so don't be put off by the weird – it could turn out to be wonderful.

Walking tour: Take an organized walking tour. Find a theme that takes your fancy – history, ghosts, architecture – a great way to not only learn more about your town but also stumble across other spots to add to your must-visit list.

Take in a show: Okay, so it might not be Broadway, but local theatres are gems that are easily overlooked. Great shows, cheaper tickets and best of all, you'll be supporting the arts in your community. Team up a show with meal out, and you've got the Big City weekend experience within a stone's throw of home.

Historic sites: A firm favorite with tourists, but locals tend to stay away as they know how horrendous the queues can get. You're missing out! Cast away your preconceptions and join the throng. Castles, cathedrals, ancient monuments – even if you think you got your fill from a school trip 20 years ago, think again. With changing exhibitions and interactive tours, there's plenty to keep both adults and children entertained.

THE GREAT OUTDOORS

You don't need far flung places to get away from it all.
It's not about distance, it's about a change of scene.

- It's very likely that there is a campsite within half an hour's journey that you have never known about because you've always looked further afield. Not the most picturesque? Who cares?! It's outdoors! Perfect for a hassle-free weekend getaway.

- Commit to switching off electronics, pack some food and a flask and head to a forest. Local government websites are great for listing woodland and parks to visit, so make good use of those resources, and find somewhere magical and unexpectedly close.

- Is water your thing, but the local pool is always too busy and the beach too far away? With water sports having a surge in popularity, investigate what your local reservoir has to offer. Most offer lessons for all ages in sailing, windsurfing, open water swimming and paddle boarding.

IN YOUR BACKYARD, LITERALLY...

The easiest expedition of all – don't leave your house!
Try these awesome activities for a quick and easy
adventure fix:

- Pitch your tent and sleep in the garden. (Throw in
  roasting marshmallows for happy kids!)
- Build a den or a treehouse.
- Cook and eat all your meals outside.
- Set up a projector in the garden and
  have a movie night. Munch
  popcorn with your friends and
  family, lounging on cushions
  under the stars.

PERSONAL ADVENTURES

Adventures aren't just about going somewhere or doing something. They can be about changing your mindset and challenging your fears – a very personal journey. Pushing your boundaries by doing something outside of your comfort zone is incredibly hard, but can reap wonderful rewards.

CONQUER A FEAR

Is there something you're afraid of? If you could overcome that fear, would it be potentially life-changing? Rather than thinking of it as an obstacle, think of it as an adventure. An adventure can be scary, but what you learn along the way and achieve at the end is well worth the challenge. Perhaps you're afraid of snakes or spiders, or would love to visit a foreign country but you're scared of flying. Think about what small steps you can take towards beating your fear. Many small steps will eventually add up to one big adventure.

44

GET STUDYING

It's very easy to think – especially as you get older and settle down with jobs and families – that it's too late to learn something new. Actually, it's never too late. Grasp an opportunity to pursue a new skill, increase your expertise in an area or simply to learn about a subject that you have always been fascinated by. Studying enriches your life, enables you to better deal with change and increases your confidence and mental aptitude – all crucial for improving your overall wellbeing. So take the plunge, book a course and set sail on a voyage of discovery.

PLANNING
GO WILD
AROUND THE WORLD
IN 80 DAYS
THE BIG ADVENTURE

TRANSFORM YOURSELF

Personal adventures can be amazingly transformative. What might you discover?

- a sense of your own personal freedom
- an understanding of your strengths and weaknesses
- new skills and talents
- a wonderful feeling of achievement
- an ability to say 'no'
- that mistakes are lessons and not disasters
- a power to inspire others.

GO BACK TO YOUR ROOTS

Your own personal adventure might mean investigating your roots. Delving into your family history will throw up fascinating facts, and give you an insight into what's made you who you are. What do you already know about your family? Talk to relatives, search the internet and visit libraries. You may even discover others are already researching part of your family tree – share what you know with them. It's all in the excitement of being a detective and slotting together the pieces of a puzzle.

This could even be the springboard for a bigger adventure. Perhaps one of your ancestors had an eventful life or was involved in a significant historical event. Could you follow in their footsteps to find out more and get a taste of what they experienced? Who knows what adventures this could lead you on?

IS SOMETHING STILL HOLDING YOU BACK?

Personal journeys are the hardest. Try these four simple steps for assessing what's stopping you from embarking on your adventure:

1 Set your goal.

2 What are the obstacles to achieving your goal?

3 Imagine the future – what would it be like if you conquer those obstacles?

4 What actions can you take to make your goal a reality?

ESCAPE THE
rat race

It's easy to forget to take time out from your busy everyday life. Yet recharging ourselves physically, mentally and spiritually is incredibly important to our health and well-being. It's not enough to switch off in front on the television – what you need is an adventure that forces you to stop, collect your thoughts and free your spirit.

TOP FIVE WAYS TO ESCAPE

Make these de-stressing activities part of your adventure:

1. Practice yoga.
2. Discover the wilderness.
3. Experience a sense of awe.
4. Meditate.
5. Write.

YOGA

Yoga may now be mainstream, but it still holds magical qualities. It can lower your blood pressure and stress levels, and boost your mood and confidence. What's not to adore about that? For an awesome adventure away from it all, book yourself on a yoga retreat. Many of these combine yoga practice with treatments and other relaxing activities. Heaven! There are some amazing and enchanting locations to choose from if you really want to go for it. How about a week in the Galgiriyawa mountains in Sri Lanka, sleeping in huts in the jungle and bathing in a lake? Or a farmhouse retreat in the Italian Umbrian hills? Near or far, get researching and start your yogic adventure.

INTO THE WILD

Get properly back to nature by heading into the wilderness. Not for the faint-hearted, but the ultimate adventure for escaping the rat race. A wilderness adventure can be a life-changing and life-affirming experience. You could find yourself pitching a tent and foraging for food in the middle of nowhere with no facilities, no power, no phone coverage, no internet ... sound good? It will push you outside of your comfort zone (quite a long way!) but what you'll learn about yourself and what you're capable of is immeasurable. If you're already a seasoned adventurer, then a wilderness trip is something you can organize yourself. For the less experienced who want a taste of the wild life, book your adventure through a knowledgeable operator who can help you get the best out of your trip.

BE AWE-INSPIRED

If you want to be reminded how small we are as humans and how amazing the world is, then get back to nature. Stand on top of a mountain, swim at the foot of a waterfall, just look up into a forest canopy – an excursion into nature is awe-inspiring. Awe allows you to connect with something bigger than yourself, and expands your usual frame of reference. It can help put your worries into perspective and create a massive tingle for all that is wonderful. Take at least a minute to gaze, relax and fully absorb the feeling of amazement. A great thing about an awe-inspiring adventure is that it could be an hour in a park or a whole week trekking through mountains. You can fit it to the time you have available, but however you do it, it will be literally awesome.

MEDITATE ON IT

We're so used to thinking, planning and organizing constantly that it can be incredibly hard to simply switch off our minds. Just like physical exercise trains the body, meditation is a wonderful way to train the mind to focus. There are many different meditation techniques, but they all have the same benefits: lower heart rate and blood pressure, less anxiety and stress and deeper relaxation. Why not enroll on a course of meditation sessions and start an adventure to explore your mind? For more intense immersion, a meditation retreat will whisk you away from all of the everyday distractions, and let you truly focus.

WRITE IT DOWN

Writing is a brilliant way to escape reality and set your imagination free on an awesome adventure. Creative writing lets you create new worlds without even leaving your front door – the size of your adventure has no limits, it doesn't even have to be within the confines of reality. You don't need to stick to fiction: try keeping a diary, journaling or blogging your travel adventures. Writing has so many benefits to your emotional and mental wellbeing. It allows you to express yourself in a healthy and safe way – think of it as talking therapy in the form of the written word. Just like traveling, writing helps you to find out about yourself and your feelings, encouraging your understanding of yourself and the world to bloom.

RAINY DAY ADVENTURES

Sometimes, you're desperate for an awesome adventure but the weather just isn't playing ball. So do you stay in? That's not the spirit of an adventurer! Rain doesn't need to stop your adventure – you just have to choose the right one.

STAYING IN

Who needs the Great Outdoors when you've got the Great Indoors? Set up camp in your own home. If you have the space, go the whole hog and pitch a tent in your living room. Shun home comforts and eat a torchlit picnic 'under canvas'.

Plan a future adventure! Use the enforced downtime to set your imagination free and think about your next vacation. Research the options and how to get there, the sights to see, how much it will cost and the fabulous food you could eat. Dream as much as you like – or make it a reality and book it!

If you love extreme sports, then do them indoors. Simple. Indoor climbing walls and ski slopes are everywhere. You can even find indoor skydiving (thrills minus the potential spills!) and caving to get your adrenaline fix.

BRAVE THE ELEMENTS

Rain brings nature to life – the smells, the colors, the squelch of mud, the splash of puddles. Get your waterproofs and rain boots on, and get out there and enjoy it. Walk through a forest, sheltered from the worst of the weather by the canopy, and let the fresh smell of the rain ooze through and awaken your senses.

Get stuck in to anything that is made more fun by lots of mud. Quad biking, mountain biking, trail running – forget the mess and embrace your inner child by getting yourself covered from head to toe.

If you're going to get wet, you might as well get completely wet and be done with it. There's something wonderfully invigorating about wild swimming – in an outdoor pool or the sea in the rain. Although obviously steer clear in thunderstorms ...

Don't avoid visiting a country in monsoon season. Realistically, the downpours only last a couple of hours. And the benefits are great – fewer crowds jostling for the best spot at sights, cleaner air and cheaper prices.

TAKE A
road trip

Nothing says adventure quite like a road trip! The freedom of the road. The wind in your hair. The anticipation of what lies ahead. It's an old cliché, but it's all about the journey, not the destination.

WHY TAKE A ROAD TRIP?

Road trips are an exhilarating adventure without needing to stray off the beaten track. You can choose what suits you based on the time you have available, your budget and who you're traveling with (great for kids but be prepared if they suffer from motion sickness!).

If you're not one for spontaneity, choose a trip that's pretty much organized for you – hire a car with a planned itinerary so you know exactly where to stop for overnight stays and the best photo opportunities. Alternatively, stick a pin in a map and just head in that direction. Either way, embrace the spirit of adventure!

TIPS FOR A PERFECT ROAD TRIP

- Spontaneous road trip or not, some planning is important to avoiding missing key sights on the way. And if you don't fancy sleeping in your car, have a few accommodation options in mind.
- Playlists and podcasts. Unless you can sustain very long conversations, then plan your in-car entertainment. Podcasts and audiobooks are a great way to while away the time, or blast out some classic road trip tracks (think Lynyrd Skynyrd's Sweet Home Alabama and Born to Be Wild by Steppenwolf). If you're traveling with kids, a tablet preloaded with movies and games is a godsend.
- Maps. Basically, have some! Especially if you want to avoid arguments. It doesn't matter if it's a paper map or GPS, just make sure they're easily to hand.
- Know the rules of the road, and avoid stressful situations such as crashing or being arrested for dangerous driving!
- Sustenance. Have snacks and drinks stashed in the car just in case the next stop is further than expected. This is especially useful to appease whining children.
- How much time do you want to spend in the car? Are you happy to drive long stretches? More frequent stops might make the trip more manageable, even if just to stretch your legs and refuel on caffeine. It's supposed to be an adventure – not torture!

FAMOUS ROUTES

If you can't think of your own route, emulate one that's already well-driven – after all, there are good reasons why they're famous! How about:

The Wild Atlantic Way (west coast of Ireland)

Ring Road (Iceland)

Cabot Trail (Canada)

North Coast 500 (Scotland)

Route 66 (USA)

Garden Route (South Africa)

South Island (New Zealand)

San Francisco to LA (USA)

Mongol Rally (12 countries – the adventure of a lifetime!)

Big Sur (USA)

Cairo to Cape Town (Africa).

TOP ROAD TRIP MOVIES

Get a taste for the open road with these fantastic road trip movies:

Little Miss Sunshine (2006)
The Motorcycle Diaries (2004)
National Lampoon's Vacation (1983)
On the Road (2012)
Planes, Trains and Automobiles (1987)
The Straight Story (1999)
Thelma and Louise (1991) (of course!)
Sideways (2004)
Diary of a Wimpy Kid: The Long Haul (2017) (one for the kids)

NOT JUST A CAR JOURNEY ...

... or about learning how to change a tire. A road trip can teach valuable life lessons. It's the spontaneous and unexpected events along the way that will make this a memorable adventure. Traveling on the road forces you to slow down and notice the details around you, opening your eyes to beauty you've not appreciated before and even giving you a new perspective on life. You'll also learn that you can't control everything – as with many awesome adventures, the only solution is to go with the flow!

GIVE SOMETHING BACK

An adventure isn't all about you! Combine an awesome adventure with giving something back to your community or the wider world. You'll be left with an enormous sense of achievement and the warm, fuzzy feeling that comes from helping others.

WHAT COULD YOU GIVE?

We've all got something to give, even if we have to think about what it is!

- Time: Multiply just a little bit of time by lots of volunteers, and it provides a project with something incredible.
- Skills and expertise: Maybe you're a marketing genius or a whizz with construction – every contribution, no matter how small, makes a massive difference to charities.
- Passion: Highly unlikely, but perhaps you don't have a useful skill to share! Passion also counts for an awful lot, so channel that enthusiasm into learning something new, at the same time as helping someone else.

WHAT COULD YOU DO?

Think about what you're interested in. If you're planning an overseas trip, here are some of the most popular options:

- Wildlife and nature conservation: Help count animals or plants for vital data collection and help protect the planet.
- Teaching: Teach a language or even basic skills for life in a school where teaching resources are stretched.
- Build something: Help build a school, a new library or toilet facilities – the things we often take for granted.

MAKE IT HAPPEN

Don't assume that volunteering adventures are free just because you're providing help! Almost every volunteer program requires you to contribute to the costs of accommodating you, plus you'll need to factor in the cost of flights and visas. You might have to embark on some fundraising activities at home to get you there, but make that part of the adventure!

JUST A WARNING ...

Do check that the project you're working with is ethical. There are hundreds of organizations offering volunteering opportunities, so ensure that they are actually helping in the way they claim. Can the organization give you evidence of how previous volunteers have made a difference? Where will the money that you pay them go? Remember that giving something back is exactly that – the needs of the project should always come above yours.

FUNDRAISING CHALLENGES

Rather than volunteering, why not make an adventure out of raising money for a charity you feel passionate about? Take a hobby like cycling to a new level by doing a sponsored ride across a country. Scale a mountain, walk the Great Wall of China, trek to Everest base camp – you don't have to make your adventure quite as big, but choose something that helps you fulfil a dream at the same time as making a huge difference to a charity.

CULINARY *adventures*

A wonderful way to have an awesome adventure is to make it an extension of a favorite hobby. If you like cycling, bike around the world. Passionate swimmer? Swim the length of the Amazon! If food is more your thing, the opportunities for turning this passion into a tasty, more sedate adventure are endless.

WHERE IN THE WORLD?

Do you love the cuisine of a particular country? Use this as a compass to launch your culinary adventure. Head to the region in France where your favorite cheese or wine is produced. Get onto the streets of Mexico to experience tacos and quesadillas at their most delicious. With a little bit of research, you can find in which areas and which restaurants you'll experience the best and most authentic local cuisine. Make meeting new people part of your adventure – word of mouth recommendations can't be beaten when it comes to food and discovering out-of-the-way gems.

TOP TEN FOODIE DESTINATIONS

1 Italy
2 China
3 France
4 Spain
5 Japan
6 India
7 Greece
8 Thailand
9 Mexico
10 US
[Source: CNN]

COOK UP A STORM

Taking a cookery course is a fantastic way to get under the skin of a cuisine, especially if the chef can give you an in-depth insight into the food and its history. Most towns and cities offer such courses for visitors, ranging from a quick morning session at your hotel to full two-week vacations in Italy taking private lessons, visiting vineyards, experiencing markets and touring factories. Such is the popularity of cooking, you can pretty much find something to suit any budget. The real adventure is being in the homeland of your chosen cuisine, being taught by those who know it and love it best.

FOR YOUR BUCKET LIST...

- Crack open whole lobsters in Maine in the US.
- Drink chilled Italian wine on a Tuscan hillside.
- Eat proper fish and chips wrapped in newspaper on a chilly English beach.
- Wash down moules and frites in Belgium with a refreshing Belgian beer.
- Enjoy melt-in-your-mouth, mouth-watering Kobe beef in Japan.
- Seek out pastel de nata – Portugal's legendary egg custard tarts – in the bakeries of Lisbon.
- Tour South Africa's Cape wine route amidst stunning mountain views.
- Mexico – the world's best destination for chocolate lovers, laying claim to cultivating cacao for nearly 4,000 years!

MUSICAL *pilgrimages*

Do you love music? It could be a particular style or artist that sends you into raptures as the notes meet your ears. So how about switching off your stereo and setting out on an awesome adventure to follow that musical passion? A musical pilgrimage will hit all the high notes!

BACK TO ITS ROOTS

Researching the roots of a musical genre opens up a whole world of fascinating history, places and people. Tracing back the history of your favorite music or your musical hero provides the perfect route to plan an adventure by. Where did it originate? Which club was the music first performed in? Where did the godfather/mother of the style grow up? It's a perfect opportunity to take a trip and immerse yourself fully in everything that you love about the music.

MUST-DO MUSICAL JOURNEYS

The Beatles: A whole tourist industry has built up around the Beatles' home city of Liverpool in the UK. Pay your respects to the real-life Penny Lane and Strawberry fields. Visit the Cavern Club where the Beatles played nearly 300 gigs or take a tour of John and Paul's childhood homes.

Graceland: Which Elvis fan doesn't dream of a trip to Graceland in Memphis, Tennessee? Elvis' home is a magnet for thousands of devoted fans every year. You may have to wade through a sea of tacky souvenirs, but you'll feel the heart of the King of Rock and Roll beating.

Country music: The home of country music – Nashville, Tennessee in the US still produces the biggest and best of this genre. Explore the evolution of the music at the Country Music Hall of Fame Museum and the Johnny Cash Museum. And, of course, spend as much time as possible enjoying live music in some of Nashville's iconic music venues.

The blues: Fancy a big musical road trip of a lifetime? Then head to the US and follow Highway 61 – the 'Blues Highway' – the route taken by African-Americans as they left the South in search of better lives in Chicago. Hear jazz in New Orleans, dance in French Louisiana, feel the roots of blues through the Delta to Clarksdale (America's most significant blues town), and then on to explore the rich musical heritage of St Louis, Davenport and Chicago.

Tango: Where else but Argentina? According to the people of Buenos Aires, tango isn't a dance, it's a lifestyle. You barely need a plan in Buenos Aires – tango is everywhere, so simply immerse yourself in this passionate way of life.

Flamenco: Grrr, feel the passion! If flamenco is your thing, then head for Spain. Seek out the most amazing festivals of music and dance – perhaps the Bienal de Flamenco in Seville or the Jerez de la Frontera Flamenco Festival – and feast on wonderful tapas to keep your energy levels up.

Classical: Austria isn't just about the Sound of Music (although there are plenty of themed tours available if you're a fan!). Take in a Mozart concert in his birthplace, Salzburg. Move on to Vienna to explore where Beethoven, Haydn, Schubert and many others lived and worked.

RECORD YOUR ADVENTURE

What better way to record your awesome musical adventure than to literally do that … record it. You obviously can't record performances without permission, so create a soundscape of memories. Focus on collecting snippets of sound that will bring memories flooding back. For example, what do you hear as you stroll down a street in New Orleans past live venues and bars? What's playing on the stereo in the taxi?

ECO-ADVENTURES

We live in a world where we're increasingly conscious of the impact we leave behind. Adventure has become less about reckless abandon and more about being responsible and sustainable. Which, of course, is a good thing! How can you ensure that your adventure makes a positive contribution to planet Earth?

WHAT IS ECOTOURISM?

The aim of ecotourism is to reduce the impact that tourism has on the environment by:

- ensuring tourism doesn't exploit the natural environment or local communities
- consulting with local communities on planned developments
- ensuring infrastructure improvements benefit local people and not just tourists.

Ultimately, it makes sure that tourism doesn't damage destinations for future generations of both locals and visitors. Eco-adventures are great for families too, teaching everyone – whatever their age – about the importance of looking after our planet. You can find anything to suit your budget – whether you want to camp on a shoestring or splash out on a luxury eco-lodge.

WHAT MAKES AN ECO-ADVENTURE?

Pretty much what it says on the tin! An eco-adventure combines an adventurous activity with environmentally responsible awareness. All eco-adventures have one common goal – appreciating and enjoying natural beauty with minimal physical impact to the area. You might find yourself:

- combatting deforestation by staying in an eco-camp in Nepal that runs on yak dung!
- cycling through the heart of Tanzania experiencing communities and landscapes only accessible on two wheels
- working on a conservation project in Costa Rica, one of the most bio-diverse countries on Earth
- experiencing the nomadic way of life trekking on horseback in Mongolia.

Do your research into the country and culture (and the travel company if you're not traveling independently) and think about how the experience will help you grow – adventure with a purpose! Remember, too, that you don't have to travel far from home for an eco-adventure, so find out what's on your doorstep, ditch the flights and reduce your carbon footprint.

HOW TO BE AN ECO-ADVENTURER

- Keep to footpaths, don't leave litter or light fires.
- Don't interfere with or feed the wildlife.
- Protect resources – use water wisely.
- Support local communities by staying in locally owned accommodation and buying from local people.
- Eat local food and drink.
- Respect local customs and traditions.

HOT TEN ECO-DESTINATIONS

Nowadays, most countries offer lots of options for eco-friendly accommodation and activities. However, below are still the classic destinations, setting the responsible tourism bar high for the rest of the world:

1 Iceland

2 The Azores

3 Costa Rica

4 New Zealand

5 Norway

6 Kenya

7 The Galapagos Islands

8 Antarctica

9 Palau

10 The Amazon Rainforest.

Map of new zealand

ANIMAL *magic*

Nothing continues to ignite our fascination and curiosity quite like animals. If you're an animal lover, then there's a myriad of ways to fill your adventure with fur, scales or feathers. Whether you want to observe from afar or get up close and personal, there's an awesome animal adventure out there for you.

ANIMAL LOVER'S BUCKET LIST

If you want to see the exotic, you will need to be prepared to travel to some far-flung destinations. These are once-in-a-lifetime opportunities though, so every hour on the road and every bit of lost sleep will be thoroughly worth it. How about this for a dream bucket list?

How to Have an Awesome Adventure

- Gorilla watching in Uganda or Rwanda.
- A Big Five African safari (that's lion, elephant, buffalo, leopard and rhino!).
- Tiger safaris in India.
- Cruising the Galapagos Islands – one of the most biologically diverse areas on the planet – with birds and animals found nowhere else on Earth.

- Whale watching in Sri Lanka.
- Meeting orangutans in Borneo.
- Bears! Polar bears in the Arctic and Grizzlies in the Rockies.

BE RESPONSIBLE!

Your adventure fast stops becoming awesome if you aren't acting in an animal's best interests. Stick to these rules:

- Don't accept local culture as an excuse for cruelty – stay away from anything you're not comfortable with.
- Avoid food that includes endangered animals or involve inhumane production.
- View wildlife in the wild where possible. Not all zoos meet satisfactory standards of care.
- Don't pay to have your photo taken with a wild animal. They may have been poorly treated to ensure they 'behave'.
- Avoid any 'trained' performances by animals, for example whales and dolphins, elephants and monkeys.
- Never buy souvenirs made from wild animals.
- Avoid riding wild animals for entertainment. They may have been trained using inappropriate methods.
- Never feed, touch, tease or provoke wild animals.

CONSERVATION

There's no better way to be responsible than to put something back into the area and wildlife you've visited by making a personal contribution to support conservation. That contribution could be in the form of a financial donation or giving up some of your time to help with a project. Some of the tasks might be very data-driven – counting animals, monitoring climate statistics – but they give you the chance to really get involved in making a difference. It certainly won't be all fluffiness, so be prepared to roll up your sleeves, whether it's shoveling elephant dung at a conservation center or preparing smelly, overripe fruit for apes!

Can't decide where to help? The WWF's priority animals for conservation efforts are: bears (including the giant panda), big cats, cetaceans (whales, dolphins and porpoises), elephants, great apes, marine turtles, rhinos, sharks and rays, sturgeons and vultures. Conserving these species will also help conserve the other species that share their habitats.

A WORD OF CAUTION...

If you're booking your adventure through a travel company, do your research. Many companies are still promoting tourist attractions that are cruel to animals. The company should have a proven record in environmental responsibility, and you need to be sure that any activities you get involved with don't have a negative impact on wildlife or support any animal suffering. Check that they adhere to ABTA's Global Welfare Guidance for Animals in Tourism. If you're in any doubt, don't use them.

GO BACK IN TIME

Have you always fancied yourself as a bit of an Indiana Jones? Then pack up your whip and set off on an awesome historical adventure. There are amazing places to visit all over the world, but don't neglect the history on your doorstep too. Go on, embrace your inner Dr Jones.

TOP DESTINATIONS FOR A HISTORY ADDICT

By no means definitive, this list could stretch to several pages! Here are a few of the real highlights for your bucket list:

1 Machu Picchu, Peru
2 Petra, Jordan
3 Angkor, Cambodia
4 Chichen Itza, Mexico
5 Khajuraho, India

6 The Pyramids at Giza, Egypt
7 Acropolis of Athens, Greece
8 Rome, Italy
9 Stonehenge, England
10 The Great Wall of China

IN THE FOOTSTEPS OF A HERO

Rather than create your own adventure, why not follow in the footsteps of a favorite historical figure?

Phileas Fogg – Okay, so a fictional character, but he traveled around the world in 80 days and that's quite an adventure! Book yourself a round-the-world ticket and try to recreate his journey.

Charles Darwin – This naturalist's odyssey onboard HMS Beagle lasted five years and took him to South America, the Galapagos Islands, Tahiti and Australia.

Marco Polo – Like this Italian explorer, follow the famous Silk Road on an epic journey through the Middle East and Central Asia to China.

Vincent van Gogh – If you love art, then retrace the steps of an artist and the locations of their famous works. Van Gogh's legacy takes you through Paris, Auvers-sur-Oise, Arles and beautiful Saint-Rémy-de-Provence in France.

DIG IT

Don't mind getting your hands dirty? Then volunteer for an archaeological dig, and help experts and scientists with the exciting task of uncovering the past. With a little bit of online research, you'll find loads of fieldwork opportunities worldwide, whether you're interested in battlefields, wreck diving, metal detecting, prehistoric or historic sites. Previous experience isn't usually required, but be prepared to work hard!

73

BE PART OF THE ACTION

Who said dressing up was just for kids? If you want your historical adventure to really get under the skin of a period, then live that history and join a re-enactment or living history society. Living history groups recreate the way that life would have been lived by wearing clothes of the time and demonstrating, for example, crafts and cookery. Re-enactors follow a script to recreate a battle or method of combat, much like a play. There's really something for everyone, whether your passion is for King Arthur or for World War II. Just be prepared for weekends in tents and an unerring commitment to historical accuracy!

TAKE IT TO THE *extreme*

When you hear the word 'adventure', do you automatically think about Lycra-clad active types climbing sheer rock faces and skiing down cliffs? Well, it's partly true! Everyone has their own idea of adventure and their own limits that they want to push. If you're an adrenaline junkie and want to take your adventure to the extreme, don't hold back!

ULTIMATE THRILL DESTINATIONS

- Costa Rica: rainforests and zip wires galore!
- New Zealand: head to the thrill capital Queenstown for extreme bungee jumping, or try white water rafting, mountain biking or skydiving.
- Switzerland: bungee jumping, river rafting, canyon jumping, skydiving, rock climbing, snowboarding and paragliding through the Alps.
- Africa: shark cage diving in South Africa, sandboarding in Namibia, white water rafting down the Zambezi River – a continent of endless opportunities!
- Nicaragua: fast becoming THE destination for volcano surfing. Yes, volcano surfing!

NEW EXTREMES

Here are some spine-tingling activities that you might not have heard of: extreme pogo, black water rafting (white water rafting but through caves in the dark), chess boxing (a round of chess followed by a round of boxing!), mountain unicycling, cliff tenting (sleep hanging in a tent anchored to the side of a mountain), handboarding (think bodyboarding but with miniature surfboards attached to your hands).

WORTH THE RISK?

If you dwell too much on the risk attached to some extreme sports, it's easy to forget the benefits! Physically, you'll improve your balance, burn an awful lot of calories and work muscles you never knew you had. There are great mental benefits too:

- Improve your self-confidence. Extreme sports require you to overcome physical and mental challenges, and that enormous sense of achievement carries over into all aspects of life.
- Fear management. Extreme sports turn fear into a positive experience. Achieve something once and your fear response decreases, helping you learn to stay calm in stressful situations.
- Increased humility. There's nothing like risk to give you a sense of your own mortality and place in the world. You learn that you're not perfect or indestructible.

IF YOU NEED INSPIRATION...

Need a push? Check out these extreme athletes at the top of their game ... Felix Baumgartner (skydiver and base jumper). Jeremy Jones (big mountain snowboarder). Lizzy Hawker (endurance athlete). Diana Nyad (long-distance swimmer). Chris Sharma (rock climber). Ed Stafford (professional adventurer and survivor). Tony Hawk (legendary skateboarder).

STAY SAFE

The risk is part of the adrenaline rush, but there are steps you can take to ensure you live to tell the tale of your awesome adventure:

- Always check out the credentials of any activity providers. Do they have the right insurance? Is the equipment well looked after? What's their safety record like?
- Use the right protective equipment. You're not there just to look good!
- Don't run before you can walk. Start with the basics and build on those for a solid foundation.
- Never do it alone. Always have someone around who can help you if need be. At the very least, they'll take great photos of you looking awesome.
- If you're traveling abroad, check that your travel insurance covers you adequately for any extreme sports activities.

ON THE BIG SCREEN

Need more inspiration, or feel safer having your awesome extreme adventure from the safety of your armchair? Check out these brilliant films based on real-life adventures to get your pulse racing:

Into the Wild (2007)

127 Hours (2010)

Touching the Void (2003)

Wild (2014)

Everest (2015)

North Face (2008)

Tracks (2013)

MAKE MONEY FROM YOUR ADVENTURE

A big adventure can be expensive, but there are ways to capitalize on it and makes some cash. Maybe you just want to recoup the cost, or perhaps you're looking at a new career option and your adventure is a stepping stone into this. There are ways to make money while enjoying your awesome adventure, but all require some hard work.

PLAN AHEAD

However tempting, don't set off on your adventure without money in your pocket – unless you want to make that the selling point of adventure! Have an idea of how long the money you leave with will last you, and have a plan in place well before it runs out. Think about what skills you have that you could utilize. Research, research, research (thank goodness for the internet).

How to Have an Awesome Adventure

VISA ALERT!

Working abroad usually requires a visa issued by the country you want to work in. Do your research before you go. Beware – work without a visa and you risk being fined, sent home or even briefly jailed!

(Planner illustration: Things to Do – Get Travel Jabs, Save Money, Close Locking Code, Check Licence/Currency Info. CHECKLIST – Passport, Visa, Tickets, Travel Insurance, Money, Health Ins)

WORKING YOUR WAY AROUND

Working in a country is a great way to immerse yourself in a culture and stash some cash. Here are some ideas to help you see the world with some money in your pocket:

Extreme sports instructor. Fruit picking and farm work. Au pairing. Teach a language. Translator. Work on a private yacht. Bar tender or waiter. Tour guide. Work on a cruise ship. Scuba diving instructor. Busker. Camp counsellor.

SELL YOUR STORY

If you're off on an unusual adventure and can write well, why not make some money by telling people about it? Admittedly, it's unlikely to earn you more than a couple of hundred, but if you're interested in a career in writing and journalism, it is a great foot in

the door. Before you go, contact publications and websites that publish stories like yours and pitch your idea. Make your pitch unique, and you will be more likely to stand out in the competitive market. If words aren't your thing but photography is, try selling the photos from your trip to an agency or stock photo website.

BLOG OR VLOG IT

It takes a while to become an online 'influencer', so this isn't the quick fix option. If you do have a large online following, you may be able to make some money from advertising on your page. If you're extremely influential, you may even see some goodies coming your way, for example accommodation in return for a write-up.

BE A DIGITAL NOMAD

The joy of modern technology is that you can pretty much work from anywhere providing there's an internet connection available. Join the ranks of the digital nomads who roam the world doing their work on a laptop on the beach! The options are endless: writing, marketing, web design, computer programming, virtual PA, professional consultant …

KEEPING A RECORD OF YOUR
adventure

Have you ever come back from an adventure full of excitement and news, and then just a week later can barely remember what you did? Or you had the most amazing experience but forgot to take your camera? How can you make sure your memories stay crystal clear for as long as possible? Find out here how to keep a record of your adventure that lasts for years.

START A BLOG

Blogs are a great way of recording your experiences online. If you're on a long adventure and you can get internet access, they're perfect for keeping your friends and family updated on what you've been up to. Best of all, setting up a blog doesn't require you to be a tech genius. There

are lots of simple – and free – online platforms available that do all the tricky stuff for you, so all you need to do is upload the content. No one expects you to be Hemingway, so simply record what you've done, seen and how you feel without feeling the pressure to write brilliantly.

KEEP A SCRAPBOOK

Tickets, postcards, leaflets, photos and receipts – scrapbooks are an easy way to record memories without having to commit to lots of writing. Gather anything that reminds you of your adventure and simply stick it into a scrapbook. It's a wonderful way to trigger memories, and works for any kind of awesome adventure, whether it be long or short.

MAP IT OUT

Marking out your adventures on a map is a fantastic way to visually represent your memories, and will make you feel like an intrepid explorer. On a large map, use pins or flags to show where you've been – add a date and a word or two to explain. If your adventure has involved a journey, then use string to link the pins, helping you to remember the path you took.

WRITE A JOURNAL

A journal requires a bit more of a time commitment than scrapbooking, but it is well worth doing if you love writing and want to record the minutiae of your adventures. Jot down your observations on the go – moments, memories, feelings – and then expand them in your journal at the end of the day. Writing everything down means you won't lose it from your memory as time passes. Re-reading a journal, like flicking through a photo album, triggers powerful memories.

WHAT IF IT doesn't go to plan?

What is it they say about best-laid plans? No matter how well you plan your adventure, sometimes things come along that stop it from being as awesome as you'd hoped. But that doesn't mean you should let it be ruined completely. Onwards and upwards!

TEN WAYS TO BOUNCE BACK WHEN THINGS GO WRONG

We invest a lot of ourselves in our plans. Even what seems like a small adventure – one that breaks an everyday routine or tackles a fear, for example – can bring huge feelings of failure if it goes wrong. And it's no less upsetting than, say, a round-the-world trip going awry. What can you do to move forward?

1 Don't panic!

2 Rather than worry about the future or the past, stick to the present and what it is in your power to do now.

3 Focus on realistic expectations for yourself.

4 Take one small step, then another, and keep moving.

5 Challenging situations can teach us something – look for the lesson to take away.

6 Appreciate the things that have gone well.

7 Keep a positive attitude by focusing on your skills and strengths.

8 Control what you can, and live with the rest.

9 Take an emotional breather and then …

10 … Plan your next adventure!

IT COULD BE WORSE

Console yourself with these tales of adventures gone wrong ...

Joseph Griffin went viral online after he got confused operating his son's GoPro. Instead of filming his trip to Las Vegas, he recorded nothing but close-ups of his face.

Adam Armstrong discovered that his girlfriend's step-dad had booked him a flight in the name of Adam West. To avoid paying the airline's $280 charge to alter the name on the ticket, he took the cheaper option of changing his name to Adam West by deed poll.

In 1982, American Larry Walters ('Lawnchair Larry') flew for 45 minutes in a homemade airship constructed from a patio chair and 45 helium-filled weather balloons, rising to an altitude of 15,000 feet. Upon landing, the airship became entangled in power lines caused a 20-minute electricity blackout in the neighborhood.

In 1999, experienced skydiver Joan Murray fell 14,500 feet after her main parachute failed to open and her reserve parachute deflated. Unlucky as she was, her luck changed when she landed on a nest of fire ants. Doctors believe that being stung by the ants saved her life as it provided the shocks to keep her heart beating through the severe body trauma.

BACK TO REALITY

Returning from an adventure – no matter how big or how small – can be a let-down, especially if your adrenaline has been surging. How can you stop the blues setting in and ride the wave of your achievements? After all, you've done it – you've had an awesome adventure!

TIPS FOR BEATING THE POST-ADVENTURE BLUES

- It is normal to feel like this! You've just done something awesome, so you will inevitably need a period of time for life to rebalance itself. If you've been away on a long adventure, readjusting to the mundane routine of everyday life can be harsh. Give it time; it will happen, and you'll start to look forwards rather than backwards again.

- Allow yourself time for a 'debrief'. It can take a while to get back to normality, so try and give yourself some time to gather your thoughts. For example, perhaps you've just conquered a fear of heights and done a skydive – if you can, take a day or two off work afterwards so that you can absorb your achievement and all the feelings that come with it. You'll feel better for it, and ready to tackle the next adventure!

How to Have an Awesome Adventure

- Remember all the great memories but don't dwell on them too much. It's very easy to mooch over photos of an experience and feel wistful that it's all over. Keep in mind the saying: 'You can't turn back the clock, but you can wind it up again'. Enjoy the memories of what you've done, but feel excitement rather than sadness and …

- … Use your feelings to drive yourself forward. What did your adventure teach you about yourself, especially what you didn't know about yourself? What changes can you make to your everyday life to use what you've learnt? It may be that you want to get involved in a charity connected to your adventure. You might even have had your eyes opened to a potential new career. Adventures are about learning new things – where will yours take you?

- Write down your next goals and plan your next adventure! Surely this is the perfect antidote to post-adventure blues? Maybe you want to take your last adventure one step further, perhaps there's a similar destination you'd like to visit. Having an awesome adventure has done something incredible for you – it's opened up a world of new opportunities. Enjoy it.

WHAT'S YOUR
next adventure?

You've done it! You've had your adventure and hopefully it was awesome. Even if you're still in the midst of your adventure – and enjoying it – it's never too early to think about another one. What's your next challenge going to be?

DE-BRIEF

Time to take a deep breath and think about what you've achieved …

- What were the best bits?
- What weren't you comfortable with? Do you want to avoid those bits in future? Or try to overcome the discomforts next time?
- What did you learn? What didn't you learn that you'd hoped you would?
- What surprised you about yourself? Did you discover hidden strengths and talents?
- An adventure is always a journey, so use what you've learnt to help you set your next challenge.

89

DELIMIT

How far do you want to push the boundaries next time?
Do you want to scale a higher mountain? Raise even more
money for your favorite charity? Or perhaps now that
you've started your yoga journey, there's a pose you want
to master. Or do you want to transfer the focus you've learnt
on your meditation course into your work life? Set your goals
and boundaries according to what you're comfortable with.
Remember that they don't need to be on a grand scale to make
you feel awesome.

DELIGHT!

Brilliant – you've got something in mind for your next adventure.
Time to let the anticipation take over, and to delight in the
planning. If you've not been used to adventures, then perhaps this
time it will be less daunting. Having an adventure is a wonderful
way to build confidence and encourage
you to go outside your comfort zone,
even if it is just inch by inch. If you're a
full-on adrenaline junkie, then the
anticipation of a new adventure
is just as thrilling as your
first. If it isn't, then
perhaps it's time to
hang up your wingsuit and
boardshorts!

PLANNER
Things to Do

Get Travel Jabs
Sort Mobile Phone Network
Check Exchange rate
Currency
Emergency cash

CHECK LIST
☐ Passport
☐ Visa
☐ Tickets
☐ Travel Insurance
☐ Money
☐ Health Ins.

A-Z OF AWESOME ADVENTURES AND ACTIVITIES

If you still need inspiration, here's a quickfire list of ideas to get your brain ticking and your imagination sparked …

A

Abseiling. Archaeological sites. Archery. Art trails. Assault courses.

B

Backpacking. Ballooning. Base jumping. Beachcombing. Bouldering. Bucket lists. Bungee jumping. Bushcraft.

C

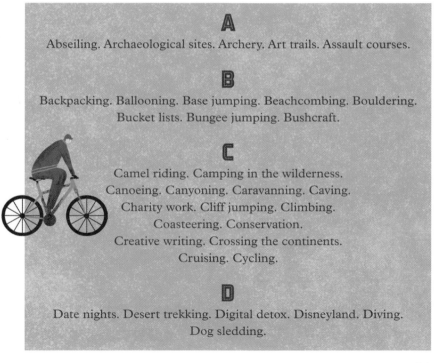

Camel riding. Camping in the wilderness. Canoeing. Canyoning. Caravanning. Caving. Charity work. Cliff jumping. Climbing. Coasteering. Conservation. Creative writing. Crossing the continents. Cruising. Cycling.

D

Date nights. Desert trekking. Digital detox. Disneyland. Diving. Dog sledding.

E

Eco-adventures. Endurance events.

F

Fell running. Festivals. Filmmaking. Flash mobs. Fly a plane.
Flyboarding. Follow a rock band on tour. Food travel. Foraging.
Forest bathing. Fundraising.

G

Geocaching. Gliding. Go-karting. Grass skiing.

H

Hang gliding. Heliskiing. High ropes. Hitchhiking (safely). Horse
riding. Hot-air ballooning.

I

Ice canoeing. Ice climbing. Indoor skydiving. Ironman/Ironwoman.

J

Jet skiing. Join the circus. Jumping (off of things safely!).

K

Kayaking. Kite fighting. Kite surfing. Kneeboarding.

L

Land yachting. Lawn mower racing. Learn something new.
Letterboxing. Living history. Longboarding.

M

Marathon. Meditation. Metal detecting. Micro-adventures.
Motorhoming. Mountain biking. Mountain unicycling.

N

Night trekking. Nordic skiing. Northern Lights.

O

Obstacle course racing. Open water swimming. Orienteering.
Overcome a fear.

P

Paddle boarding. Paintballing. Parachuting.
Paragliding. Parkour. Photography.

Q

Quad biking. Quadrathlon.

R

Rafting. Rappelling. Re-enactments. Research your family tree.
Retreats. Road trips. Rock climbing.

S

Safari. Scavenger hunts. Set a new record. Skinny dipping.
Skydiving. Slacklining. Sleep on a beach. Snorkeling. Spa.
Stargazing. Stay up all night. Storm chasing. Study something new.
Surfing. Swim with sharks. Swoop swinging.

T

Theme parks. Tourist trails. Trail running.
Trans-Siberian railway. Triathlons.
Treasure hunts.

U

Ultra-marathons. Underwater orienteering.

V

Vert skateboarding. Vintage car racing.
Volcano boarding. Volunteering.

W

Wakeboarding. Walk down memory lane. Walking.
Whale spotting. White water rafting. Wild swimming.
Wilderness. Wing walking.

X

Xtreme sports!

Y

Yachting. Saying 'Yes' rather than 'No'. Yoga.

Z

Zip lining. Zorbing.

YOUR OWN AWESOME PLANS AND IDEAS

Use this space to jot down adventurous ideas of your own – think as big or as small as you like. It's your adventure. Dream wonderful things and plan exciting times!

MY BUCKET LIST

DREAM DESTINATIONS

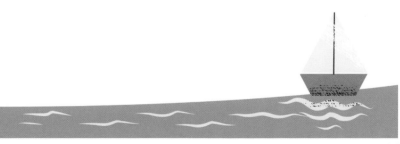

WHAT DO I WANT TO ACHIEVE?

MY BUDGET

USEFUL WEBSITES